Kristen Suzanne's
EASY
Raw Vegan
Sides & Snacks

Delicious & Easy Raw Food Recipes
for Side Dishes, Snacks,
Spreads, Dips, Sauces & Breakfast

by Kristen Suzanne

*Green
Butterfly
Press*

Scottsdale, Arizona

OTHER BOOKS BY KRISTEN SUZANNE

- *Kristen's Raw: The EASY Way to Get Started & Succeed at the Raw Food Vegan Diet & Lifestyle*
- *Kristen Suzanne's EASY Raw Vegan Entrees*
- *Kristen Suzanne's EASY Raw Vegan Desserts*
- *Kristen Suzanne's EASY Raw Vegan Soups*
- *Kristen Suzanne's EASY Raw Vegan Salads & Dressings*
- *Kristen Suzanne's EASY Raw Vegan Smoothies, Juices, Elixirs & Drinks (includes wine drinks!)*
- *Kristen Suzanne's EASY Raw Vegan Holidays*
- *Kristen Suzanne's EASY Raw Vegan Dehydrating*
- *Kristen Suzanne's Ultimate Raw Vegan Hemp Recipes*

COMING SOON

- *Kristen Suzanne's Raw Vegan Diet for EASY Weight Loss*
- *Kristen Suzanne's Ultimate Raw Vegan Chocolate Recipes*

For details, Raw Food resources, and Kristen's free Raw Food newsletter, please visit:

KristensRaw.com

For information on excerpting, reprinting or licensing portions of this book, please write to info@greenbutterflypress.com.

Green Butterfly Press
19550 N. Gray Hawk Drive, Suite 1042
Scottsdale, AZ 85255 USA

Library of Congress Control Number: 2008941403
Library of Congress Subject Heading:
1. Cookery (Natural foods) 2. Raw foods

ISBN: 978-0-9817556-5-6

1.3

CONTENTS

CHAPTER 1

RAW BASICS

NOTE: "Raw Basics" is a brief introduction to Raw for those who are new to the subject. It is the same in all of my recipe books. If you have recently read this section in one of them, you may wish to skip to Chapter 2.

WHY RAW?

Living the Raw vegan lifestyle has made me a more effective person... in everything I do. I get to experience pure, sustainable all-day-long energy. My body is in perfect shape and I gain strength and endurance in my exercise routine with each passing day. My relationships are the best they've ever been, because I'm happy and I love myself and my life. My headaches have ceased to exist, and my skin glows with the radiance of brand new life, which is exactly how I feel. Raw vegan is the best thing that has ever happened to me.

Whatever your passion is in life (family, business, exercise, meditation, hobbies, etc.), eating Raw vegan will take it to unbelievable new heights. Raw vegan food offers you the most amazing benefits—physically, mentally, and spiritually. It is *the* ideal choice for your food consumption if you want to become the healthiest and best "you" possible. Raw vegan food is for people who want to live longer while feeling younger. It's for people who want to feel vibrant and alive, and want to enjoy life like never before. All I ever have to say to someone is, "Just try it for yourself." It will change your life. From simple to gourmet, there's always something for everyone, and it's delicious. Come into the world of Raw with me, and experience for yourself the most amazing health *ever*.

Are you ready for your new lease on life? The time is now. Let's get started!

SOME GREAT THINGS TO KNOW BEFORE DIVING INTO THESE RECIPES

Organic Food

I use organic produce and products for pretty much everything. There are very few exceptions, and that would be if the recipe called for something I just can't get organic such as jicama, young Thai coconuts, certain seasonings, or any random ingredient that my local health food store is not able to procure from an organic grower for whatever reason.

If you think organic foods are too expensive, then start in baby steps and buy a few things at a time. Realize that you're going to be spending less money in the long run on health problems as your health improves, and going organic is one way to facilitate that. I find that once people learn about the direct cause-and-effect relationship between non-organic food and illnesses such as cancer, the relatively small premium you pay for organic becomes a trivial non-issue. Your health is worth it!

Choosing organically grown foods is one of the most important choices we can make. The more people who choose organic, the lower the prices will be in the long run. Vote with your dollar! Here is something I do to help further this cause and you can, too... whenever I eat at a restaurant I always write on the bill, "I would eat here more if you served organic food." Can you imagine what would happen if we all did this?

It's essential to use organic ingredients for many reasons:

1. The health benefits – superior nutrition, reduced intake of chemicals and heavy metals and decreased exposure to carcinogens. Organic food has been shown to have up to 300% more nutrition than conventionally grown, non-organic produce.

2. To have the very best tasting food ever! I've had people tell me in my classes that they never knew vegetables tasted so good – and it's because I only use organic.

3. Greater variety of heirloom fruits and vegetables.

4. Cleaner rivers and waterways for our earth, along with minimized topsoil erosion.

Going Organic on a Budget

Going organic on a budget is not impossible. Here are things to keep in mind that will help you afford it:

1. Buy in bulk. Ask the store you frequent if they'll give you a deal for buying certain foods by the case. (Just make sure it's a case of something that you can go through in a timely fashion so it doesn't go to waste). Consider this for bananas or greens especially if you drink lots of smoothies or green juice, like I do.

2. See if local neighbors, family or friends will share the price of getting cases of certain foods. When you do this, you can go beyond your local grocery store and contact great places (which deliver nationally) such as Boxed Greens (BoxedGreens.com) or Diamond Organics (DiamondOrganics.com). Maybe they'll extend a discount if your order goes above a certain

amount or if you get certain foods by the case. It never hurts to ask.

3. Pay attention to organic foods that are not very expensive to buy relative to the conventional prices (bananas, for example). Load up on those.

4. Be smart when picking what you buy as organic. Some conventionally grown foods have higher levels of pesticides than others. For those, go organic. Then, for foods that are not sprayed as much, you can go conventional. Avocados, for example, aren't sprayed too heavily so you could buy those as conventional. Here is a resource that keeps an updated list:

   foodnews.org/walletguide.php

5. Buy produce that is on sale. Pay attention to which organic foods are on sale for the week and plan your menu around that. Every little bit adds up!

6. Grow your own sprouts. Load up on these for salads, soups, and smoothies. Very inexpensive. Buy the organic seeds in the bulk bins at your health food store or buy online and grow them yourself. Fun!

7. Buy organic seeds/nuts in bulk online and freeze. Nuts and seeds typically get less expensive when you order in bulk from somewhere like Sun Organic (SunOrganic.com). Take advantage of this and freeze them (they'll last the year!). Do the same with dried fruits/dates/etc. And remember, when you make a recipe that calls for expensive nuts, you can often easily replace them with a less expensive seed such as sunflower or pumpkin seeds.

8. Buy seasonally; hence, don't buy a bunch of organic berries out of season (i.e., eat more apples and bananas in the fall and winter). Also, consider buying frozen organic fruits, especially when they're on sale!

9. Be content with minimal variety. Organic spinach banana smoothies are inexpensive. So, having this most mornings for your breakfast can save you money. You can change it up for fun by adding cinnamon one day, nutmeg another, vanilla extract yet another. Another inexpensive meal or snack is a spinach apple smoothie. Throw in a date or some raisins for extra pizazz. It helps the budget when you make salads, smoothies, and soups with ingredients that tend to be less expensive such as carrots (year round), bananas (year round), zucchini and cucumbers (in the summer), etc.

Kristen Suzanne's Tip: A Note About Herbs

Hands down, fresh herbs taste the best and have the highest nutritional value. While I recommend fresh herbs whenever possible, you can substitute dried herbs if necessary. But do so in a ratio of:

3 parts fresh to 1 part dried

Dried herbs impart a more concentrated flavor, which is why you need less of them. For instance, if your recipe calls for three tablespoons of fresh basil, you'll be fine if you use one tablespoon of dried basil instead.

The Infamous Salt Question: What Kind Do I Use?

All life on earth began in the oceans, so it's no surprise that organisms' cellular fluids chemically resemble sea water. Saltwater in the ocean is "salty" due to many, many minerals, not just sodium chloride. We need these minerals, not coincidentally, in roughly the same proportion that they exist in... guess where?... the ocean! (You've just gotta love Mother Nature.)

So when preparing food, I always use sea salt, which can be found at any health food store. Better still is sea salt that was deposited into salt beds before the industrial revolution started spewing toxins into the world's waterways. My personal preference is Himalayan Crystal Salt, fine granules. It's mined high in the mountains from ancient sea-beds, has a beautiful pink color, and imparts more than 84 essential minerals into your diet. You can use either the Himalayan crystal variety or Celtic Sea Salt, but I would highly recommend sticking to at least one of these two. You can buy Himalayan crystal salt through KristensRaw.com/store.

Kristen Suzanne's Tip: Start Small with Strong Flavors

FLAVORS AND THEIR STRENGTH

There are certain flavors and ingredients that are particularly strong, such as garlic, ginger, onion, and salt. It's important to observe patience here, as these are flavors that can be loved or considered offensive, depending on who is eating the food. I know people who want the maximum amount of salt called for in a recipe and I know some who are highly sensitive to it. Therefore, to make the best possible Raw experience for you, I recommend starting on the "small end" especially with ingredients like garlic, ginger, strong savory herbs and seasonings, onions (any variety), citrus, and even salt. If I've given you a range in a recipe, for instance *1/4 - 1/2 teaspoon Himalayan crystal salt* then I recommend starting with the smaller amount, and then tasting it. If you don't love it, then add a little more of that ingredient and taste it again. Start small. It's worth the extra 60 seconds it might take you to do this. You might end up using less, saving it for the next recipe you make and voila, you're saving a little money.

Lesson #1: It's very hard to correct any flavors of excess, so start small and build.

Lesson #2: Write it down. When an ingredient offers a "range" for itself, write down the amount you liked best. If you use an "optional" ingredient, make a note about that as well.

One more thing to know about some strong flavors like the ones mentioned above... with Raw food, these flavors can intensify the finished product as each day passes. For example, the garlic in your soup, on the day you made it, might be perfect. On day two, it's still really great but a little stronger in flavor. And by day three, you might want to carry around your toothbrush or a little chewing gum!

HERE IS A TIP TO HELP CONTROL THIS

If you're making a recipe in advance, such as a dressing or soup that you won't be eating until the following day or even the day after that, then hold off on adding some of the strong seasonings until the day you eat it (think garlic and ginger). Or, if you're going to make the dressing or soup in advance, use less of the strong seasoning, knowing that it might intensify on its own by the time you eat it. This isn't a huge deal because it doesn't change that dramatically, but I mention it so you won't be surprised, especially when serving a favorite dish to others.

Kristen Suzanne's Tip: Doubling Recipes

More often than not, there are certain ingredients and flavors that you don't typically double in their entirety, if you're making a double or triple batch of a recipe. These are strong-flavored ingredients similar to those mentioned above (salt, garlic, ginger, herbs, seasoning, etc). A good rule of thumb is this: For a double batch, use 1.5 times the amount for certain ingredients. Taste it and see if you need the rest. For instance, if I'm making a "double batch" of soup, and the normal recipe calls for 1 tablespoon of Himalayan crystal salt, then I'll put in 1 1/2 tablespoons to start, instead of two. Then, I'll taste it and add the remaining 1/2 tablespoon, if necessary.

This same principle is not necessarily followed when dividing a recipe in half. Go ahead and simply divide in half, or by whatever amount you're making. If there is a range for a particular ingredient provided, I still recommend that you use the smaller amount of an ingredient when dividing. Taste the final product and then decide whether or not to add more.

My recipes provide a variety of yields, as you'll see below. Some recipes make 2 servings and some make 4 - 6 servings. For those of you making food for only yourself, then simply cut the recipes making 4 - 6 servings in half. Or, as I always do... I make the larger serving size and then I have enough food for a couple of meals. If a recipe yields 2 servings, I usually double it for the same reason.

Kristen Suzanne's Tip: Changing Produce

"But I made it exactly like this last time! Why doesn't it taste the same?"

Here is something you need to embrace when preparing Raw vegan food. Fresh produce can vary in its composition of water, and even flavor, to some degree. There are times I've made marinara sauce and, to me, it was the perfect level of sweetness in the finished product. Then, the next time I made it, you would have thought I added a smidge of sweetener. This is due to the fact that fresh Raw produce can have a slightly different taste from time to time when you make a recipe (only ever so slightly, so don't be alarmed). *Aahhh, here is the silver lining!* This means you'll never get bored living the Raw vegan lifestyle because your recipes can change a little in flavor from time to time, even though you followed the same recipe. Embrace this natural aspect of produce and love it for everything that it is. ☺

This is much less of an issue with cooked food. Most of the water is taken out of cooked food, so you typically get the same flavors and experience each and every time. Boring!

Kristen Suzanne's Tip: Ripeness and Storage for Your Fresh Produce

1. I never use green bell peppers because they are not "ripe." This is why so many people have a hard time digesting them (often "belching" after eating them). To truly experience the greatest health, it's important to eat fruits and vegetables at their peak ripeness. Therefore, make sure you only use red, orange, or yellow bell peppers. Store these in your refrigerator.

2. A truly ripe banana has some brown freckles or spots on the peel. This is when you're supposed to eat a banana. Store these on your countertop away from other produce, because bananas give off a gas as they ripen, which will affect the ripening process of your other produce. And, if you have a lot of bananas, split them up. This will help prevent all of your bananas from ripening at once.

3. Keep avocados on the counter until they reach ripeness (when their skin is usually brown in color and if you gently squeeze it, it "gives" just a little). At this point, you can put them in the refrigerator where they'll last up to a week longer. If you keep ripe avocados on the counter, they'll only last another couple of days. Avocados, like bananas, give off a gas as they ripen, which will affect the ripening process of your other produce. Let them ripen away from your other produce. And, if you have a lot of avocados, separate them. This will help prevent all of your avocados from ripening at once.

4. Tomatoes are best stored on your counter. Do not put them in the refrigerator or they'll get a "mealy" texture.

5. Pineapple is ripe for eating when you can gently pull a leaf out of the top of it. Therefore, test your pineapple for ripeness at the store to ensure you're buying the sweetest one possible. Just pull one of the leaves out from the top. After 3 to 4 attempts on different leaves, if you can't gently take one of them out, then move on to another pineapple.

6. Stone fruits (fruits with pits, such as peaches, plums, and nectarines), bananas and avocados all continue to ripen after being picked.

7. I have produce ripening all over my house. Sounds silly maybe, but I don't want it crowded on my kitchen countertop. I move it around and turn it over daily.

For a more complete list of produce ripening tips, check out my book, *Kristen's Raw,* available at Amazon.com.

Kristen Suzanne's Tip: Proper Dehydration Techniques

Dehydrating your Raw vegan food at a low temperature is a technique that warms and dries the food while preserving its nutritional integrity. When using a dehydrator, it is recommended that you begin the dehydrating process at a temperature of 130 - 140 degrees for about an hour. Then, lower the temperature to 105 degrees for the remaining time of dehydration. Using a high temperature such as 140 degrees, *in the initial stages of dehydration,* does not destroy the nutritional value of the food. During this initial phase, the food does the most "sweating" (releasing moisture), which cools the food. Therefore, while the temperature of the air circulating *around* the food is about 140 degrees, the food itself is much cooler. These directions apply only when using an Excalibur Dehydrator because of their Horizontal-Airflow Drying System. Furthermore, I am happy to only recommend Excalibur dehydrators because of their first-class products and customer service. For details, visit the *Raw Kitchen Essential Tools* section of my website at KristensRaw.com/store.

MY YIELD AND SERVING AMOUNTS NOTED IN THE RECIPES

Each recipe in this book shows an approximate amount that the recipe yields (the quantity it makes). I find that "one serving" to me might be considered two servings to someone else, or vice versa. Therefore, I tried to use an "average" when listing the serving amount. Don't let that stop you from eating a two-serving dish in one sitting, if it seems like the right amount for you. It simply depends on how hungry you are.

WHAT IS THE DIFFERENCE BETWEEN CHOPPED, DICED, AND MINCED?

Chop

This gives relatively uniform cuts, but doesn't need to be perfectly neat or even. You'll often be asked to chop something before putting it into a blender or food processor, which is why it doesn't have to be uniform size since it'll be getting blended or pureed.

Dice

This produces a nice cube shape, and can be different sizes, depending on which you prefer. This is great for vegetables.

Mince

This produces an even, very fine cut, typically used for fresh herbs, onions, garlic and ginger.

Julienne

This is a fancy term for long, rectangular cuts.

WHAT EQUIPMENT DO I NEED FOR MY NEW RAW FOOD KITCHEN?

I go into much more detail regarding the perfect setup for your Raw vegan kitchen in my book, *Kristen's Raw,* which is a must read for anybody who wants to learn the easy ways to succeed with living the Raw vegan lifestyle. Here are the main pieces of equipment you'll want to get you going:

1. An excellent chef's knife (6 - 8 inches in length – non-serrated). Of everything you do with Raw food, you'll be chopping and cutting the most, so invest in a great knife. This truly makes doing all the chopping really fun!

2. Blender

3. Food Processor (get a 7 or 10-cup or more)

4. Juicer

5. Spiralizer or Turning Slicer

6. Dehydrator – Excalibur® is the best company by far and is available at KristensRaw.com

7. Salad spinner

8. Other knives (paring, serrated)

For links to online retailers that sell my favorite kitchen tools and foods, visit KristensRaw.com/store.

SOAKING AND DEHYDRATING NUTS AND SEEDS

This is an important topic. When using nuts and seeds in Raw vegan foods, you'll find that recipes sometimes call for them to be "soaked" or "soaked and dehydrated." Here is the low-down on the importance and the difference between the two.

Why should you soak your nuts and seeds?

Most nuts and seeds come packed by Mother Nature with enzyme inhibitors, rendering them harder to digest. These inhibitors essentially shut down the nuts' and seeds' metabolic activity, rendering them dormant—for as long as they need to be—until they detect a moisture-rich environment that's suitable for germination (e.g., rain). By soaking your nuts and seeds, you trick the nuts into "waking up," shutting off the inhibitors so that the enzymes can become active. This greatly enhances the nuts' digestibility for you and is highly recommended if you want to experience Raw vegan food in the healthiest way possible.

14

Even though you'll want to soak the nuts to activate their enzymes, before using them, you'll need to re-dry them and grind them down anywhere from coarse to fine (into a powder almost like flour), depending on the recipe. To dry them, you'll need a dehydrator. (If you don't own a dehydrator yet, then, if a recipe calls for "soaked and dehydrated," just skip the soaking part; you can use the nuts or seeds in the dry form that you bought them).

Drying your nuts (but not yet grinding them) is a great thing to do before storing them in the freezer or refrigerator (preferably in glass mason jars). They will last a long time and you'll always have them on hand, ready to use.

In my recipes, always use nuts and seeds that are "soaked and dehydrated" (that is, *dry*) unless otherwise stated as "soaked" (wet).

Some nuts and seeds don't have to follow the enzyme inhibitor rule; therefore, they don't need to be soaked. These are:

- Macadamia nuts
- Brazil nuts
- Pine nuts
- Hemp seeds
- Most cashews

An additional note... there are times when the recipe will call for soaking, even though it's for a type of nut or seed without enzyme inhibitors, such as Brazil nuts. The logic behind this is to help *soften* the nuts so they blend into a smoother texture, especially if you don't have a high-powered blender. This is helpful when making nut milks, soups and sauces.

Instructions for "Soaking" and "Soaking and Dehydrating" Nuts

"Soaking"

The general rule to follow: Any nuts or seeds that require soaking can be soaked overnight (6 - 10 hours). Put the required amount of nuts or seeds into a bowl and add enough water to cover by about an inch or so. Set them on your counter overnight. The following morning, or 6 - 10 hours after you soaked them, drain and rinse them. They are now ready to eat or use in a recipe. At this point, they need to be refrigerated in an airtight container (preferably a glass mason jar) and they'll have a shelf life of about 3 days maximum. Only soak the amount you're going to need or eat, unless you plan on dehydrating them right away.

A note about flax seeds and chia seeds... these don't need to be soaked if your recipe calls for grinding them into a powder. Some recipes will call to soak the seeds in their "whole-seed" form, before making crackers and bread, because they create a very gelatinous and binding texture when soaked. You can soak flax or chia seeds in a ratio of one-part seeds to two-parts water, and they can be soaked for as short as 1 hour and up to 12 hours. At this point, they are ready to use (don't drain them). Personally, when I use flax seeds, I usually grind them and don't soak them. It's hard for your body to digest "whole" flax seeds, even if they are soaked. It's much easier for your body to assimilate the nutrients when they're ground to a flax meal.

"Soaking and Dehydrating"

Follow the same directions for soaking. Then, after draining and rinsing the nuts, spread them out on a mesh dehydrator sheet and dehydrate them at 140 degrees for one hour. Lower the temperature to 105 degrees and dehydrate them until they're completely dry, which can take up to 24 hours.

Please note, all nuts and seeds called for in my recipes will always be "Raw and Organic" and "Soaked and Dehydrated" unless the recipe calls for soaking.

ALMOND PULP

Some of my recipes call for "almond pulp," which is really easy to make. After making your fresh almond milk (see "*Nut Milk*" recipe, below) and straining it through a "nut milk bag," (available at NaturalZing.com or you can use a paint strainer bag from the hardware store – much cheaper), you will find a nice, soft pulp inside the bag. Turn the bag inside out and flatten the pulp out onto a paraflex dehydrator sheet with a spatula or your hand. Dehydrate the pulp at 140 degrees for one hour, then lower the temperature to 105 degrees and continue dehydrating until the almond pulp is dry (up to 24 hours). Break the pulp into chunks and store in the freezer until you're ready to use it. Before using the almond pulp, grind it into a flour in your blender or food processor.

SOY LECITHIN

Some recipes (desserts, in particular) will call for soy lecithin, which is extracted from soybean oil. This optional ingredient is not Raw. If you use soy lecithin, I highly recommend using a brand that is "non-GMO," meaning it was processed without any genetically modified ingredients (a great brand is Health Alliance®). Soy lecithin helps your dessert (cheesecake, for example) maintain a firmer texture.

That said, it's certainly not necessary. If an amount isn't suggested, a good rule of thumb is to use 1 teaspoon per 1 cup total recipe volume.

ICE CREAM FLAVORINGS

When making Raw vegan ice cream, it's better to use alcohol-free extracts so they freeze better.

SWEETENERS

The following is a list of sweeteners that you might see used in my recipes. It's important to know that the healthiest sweeteners are fresh whole fruits, including fresh dates. That said, dates sometimes compromise texture in recipes. As a chef, I look for great texture, and as a health food advocate, I lean towards fresh dates. But as a consultant helping people embrace a Raw vegan lifestyle, I'm also supportive of helping them transition, which sometimes means using raw agave nectar, or some other easy-to-use sweetener that might not have the healthiest ranking in the Raw food world, but is still much healthier than most sweeteners used in the Standard American Diet.

Most of my recipes can use pitted dates in place of raw agave nectar. There is some debate among Raw food enthusiasts as to whether agave nectar is Raw. The company I use (Madhava®) claims to be Raw and says they do not heat their Raw agave nectar above 118 degrees. If however, you still want to eat the healthiest of sweeteners, then bypass the raw agave nectar and use pitted dates. In most recipes, you can simply substitute 1 - 2 pitted dates for 1 tablespoon of raw agave nectar. Dates won't give you a super creamy texture, but the texture can be improved by making a "date paste" (pureeing pitted and soaked dates – with their soak water, plus some additional water, if necessary – in a food processor fitted with the "S" blade). This, of course, takes a little extra time.

If using raw agave nectar is easier and faster for you, then go ahead and use it; just be sure to buy the Raw version that says they don't heat the agave above 118 degrees (see KristensRaw.com/store for links to this product). And, again, if you're looking to go as far as you can on the spectrum of health, then I recommend using pitted dates. Most of my recipes say raw agave nectar because that is most convenient for people.

Agave Nectar

There are a variety of agave nectars on the market, but again, not all of them are Raw. Make sure it is labeled "Raw" on the bottle *as well as claiming that it isn't processed above 118 degrees*. Just because the label says "Raw" does not necessarily mean it is so... do a double check and make sure it also claims not to be heated above the 118 degrees cut-off. Agave nectar is noteworthy for having a low glycemic index.

Dates

Dates are probably the healthiest of sweeteners, because they're a fresh whole food. Fresh organic dates are filled with nutrition, including calcium and magnesium. I like to call dates, "Nature's Candy."

Feel free to use dates instead of agave or honey in Raw vegan recipes. If a recipe calls for 1/2 cup of raw agave, then you can substitute with approximately 1/2 cup of pitted dates. You can also make your own date sugar by dehydrating pitted dates and then grinding them down. This is a great alternative to Rapadura®.

Honey

Most honey is technically raw, but it is not vegan by most definitions of "vegan" because it is produced by animals, who therefore are at risk of being mistreated. While honey does not have the health risks associated with animal byproducts such as eggs or dairy, it can spike the body's natural sugar levels. Agave nectar has a lower, healthier glycemic index and can replace any recipe you find that calls for honey, in a 1 to 1 ratio.

Maple Syrup

Maple syrup is made from boiled sap of the maple tree. It is not considered Raw, but some people still use it as a sweetener in certain dishes.

Rapadura®

This is a dried sugarcane juice, and it's not Raw. It is, however, an unrefined and unbleached organic whole-cane sugar. It imparts a nice deep sweetness to your recipes, even if you only use a little. Feel free to omit it if you'd like to adhere to a strictly Raw program. You can substitute Rapadura with home-made date sugar (see Dates above).

Stevia

This is from the leaf of the stevia plant. It has a sweet taste and doesn't elevate blood sugar levels. It's very sweet, so you'll want to use much less stevia than you would any other sweetener. My mom actually grows her own stevia. It's a great addition in fresh smoothies, for example, to add some sweetness without the calories. You can use the white powdered or liquid version from the store, but these are not Raw. When possible, the best way to have stevia is grow it yourself.

Yacon Syrup

This sweetener has a low glycemic index, making it very attractive to some people. It has a molasses-type flavor that is nice and rich. You can replace raw agave with this sweetener in my recipes, but make sure to get the Raw variety, available at NaturalZing.com. They offer a few different yacon syrups, including one in particular that is not heat-treated. Be sure to choose that one.

SUN-DRIED TOMATOES

By far, the best sun-dried tomatoes are those you make yourself with a dehydrator. If you don't have a dehydrator, make sure you buy the "dry" sun-dried tomatoes, usually found in the bulk section of your health food market. Don't buy the kind that are packed in a jar of oil.

Also... don't buy sun-dried tomatoes if they're really dark (almost black) because these just don't taste as good. Again, I recommend making them yourself if you truly want the freshest flavor possible. It's really fun to do!

EATING WITH YOUR EYES

Most of us, if not all, naturally eat with our eyes before taking a bite of food. So, do yourself a favor and make your eating experience the best ever with the help of a simple, gorgeous presentation. Think of it this way, with real estate, it's always *location, location, location,* right? Well, with food, it's always *presentation, presentation, presentation.*

Luckily, Raw food does this on its own with all of its naturally vibrant and bright colors. But I take it even one step farther—I use my best dishes when I eat. I use my beautiful wine glasses for my smoothies and juices. I use my fancy goblets for many of my desserts. Why? Because I'm worth it. And, so are you! Don't save your good china just for company. Believe me, you'll notice the difference. Eating well is an attitude, and when you take care of yourself, your body will respond in kind.

ONLINE RESOURCES FOR GREAT PRODUCTS

For a complete and detailed list of my favorite kitchen tools, products, and various foods (all available online), please visit: KristensRaw.com/store.

BOOK RECOMMENDATIONS

I highly recommend reading the following life-changing books.

- *Diet for a New America*, by John Robbins
- *The Food Revolution*, by John Robbins
- *The China Study*, by T. Colin Campbell
- *Skinny Bitch*, by Rory Freedman

MEASUREMENT CONVERSIONS

1 tablespoon = 3 teaspoons

1 ounce = 2 tablespoons

1/4 cup = 4 tablespoons

1/3 cup = 5 1/3 tablespoons

1 cup

= 8 ounces

= 16 tablespoons

= 1/2 pint

1/2 quart

= 1 pint

= 2 cups

1 gallon

= 4 quarts

= 8 pints

= 16 cups

= 128 ounces

BASIC RECIPES TO KNOW

Nourishing Rejuvelac

Yield 1 gallon

Rejuvelac is a cheesy-tasting liquid that is rich in enzymes and healthy flora to support a healthy intestine and digestion.

Get comfortable making this super easy recipe because its use goes beyond just drinking it between meals.

1 cup soft wheat berries, rye berries, or a mixture

water

Place the wheat berries in a half-gallon jar and fill the jar with water. Screw the lid on the jar and soak the wheat berries overnight(10 - 12 hours) on your counter. The next morning, drain and rinse them. Sprout the wheat berries for 2 days, draining and rinsing 1 - 2 times a day.

Then, fill the jar with purified water and screw on the lid, or cover with cheesecloth secured with a rubber band. Allow to ferment for 24 - 36 hours, or until the desired tartness is achieved. It should have a cheesy, almost tart/lemony flavor and scent.

Strain your rejuvelac into another glass jar and store in the refrigerator for up to 5 - 7 days. For a second batch using the same sprouted wheat berries, fill the same jar of already sprouted berries with water again, and allow to ferment for 24 hours. Strain off the rejuvelac as you did the time before this. You can do this process yet again, noting that each time the rejuvelac gets a little weaker in flavor.

Enjoy 1/4 - 1 cup of *Nourishing Rejuvelac* first thing in the morning and/or between meals. It's best to start with a small amount and work your way up as your body adjusts.

Suggestion:

- For extra nutrition and incredible flavor, *Nourishing Rejuvelac* can be used in various recipes such as Raw vegan cheeses, desserts, smoothies, soups, dressings and more. Simply use it in place of the water required by the recipe.

Crème Fraiche

Yield approximately 2 cups

> 1 cup cashews, soaked 1 hour, drained, and rinsed
>
> 1/4 - 1/2 cup *Nourishing Rejuvelac* (see above)
>
> 1 - 2 tablespoons raw agave nectar

Blend the ingredients until smooth. Store in an airtight glass mason jar for up to 5 days. This freezes well, so feel free to make a double batch for future use.

Nut/Seed Milk (regular)

Yield 4 - 5 cups

The creamiest nut/seed milk traditionally comes from hemp seeds, cashews, pine nuts, Brazil nuts or macadamia nuts, although I'm also a huge fan of milks made from walnuts, pecans, hazelnuts, almonds, sesame seeds, and others.

This recipe does not include a sweetener, but when I'm in the mood for a little sweetness, I add a couple of pitted dates or a squirt of raw agave nectar. Yum!

> 1 1/2 cups nuts, soaked 6 - 12 hours, drained and rinsed
>
> 3 1/4 cups water
>
> pinch Himalayan crystal salt, optional

Blend the ingredients until smooth and deliciously creamy. For an even *extra creamy* texture, strain your nut/seed milk through a nut milk bag.

Sweet Nut/Seed Cream (thick)

Yield 2 - 3 cups

> 1 cup nuts or seeds, soaked 6 - 8 hours, drained and rinsed
>
> 1 - 1 1/2 cups water, more if needed
>
> 2 - 3 tablespoons raw agave nectar or 2 - 3 dates, pitted
>
> 1/2 teaspoon vanilla extract, optional

Blend all of the ingredients until smooth.

Raw Mustard

Yield approximately 1 1/2 - 2 cups

> 1 - 2 tablespoons yellow mustard seeds (depending on how "hot" you want it), soaked 1 - 2 hours
>
> 1 1/2 cups extra virgin olive oil or hemp oil
>
> 1 1/2 tablespoons dry mustard powder
>
> 2 tablespoons apple cider vinegar
>
> 2 tablespoons fresh lemon juice
>
> 3 dates, pitted and soaked 30-minutes, drained
>
> 1/2 cup raw agave nectar
>
> 1 teaspoon Himalayan crystal salt
>
> pinch turmeric

Blend all of the ingredients together until smooth. It might be very thick, so if you want, add some water or oil to help thin it out. Adding more oil will help reduce the "heat" if it's too spicy for your taste.

Variation:

- *Honey Mustard Version:* Add another 1/3 cup raw agave nectar (or more, depending on how sweet you want it)

My Basic Raw Mayonnaise

Yield about 2 1/2 cups

People tell me all the time how much they like this recipe.

1 cup cashews, soaked 1 - 2 hours, drained
1/2 teaspoon paprika
2 cloves garlic
1 teaspoon onion powder
3 tablespoons fresh lemon juice
1/4 cup extra virgin olive oil or hemp oil
2 tablespoons parsley, chopped
2 tablespoons water, if needed

Blend all of the ingredients, except the parsley, until creamy. Pulse in the parsley. *My Basic Raw Mayonnaise* will stay fresh for up to one week in the refrigerator.

CHAPTER 2

SIDE DISHES

Side dishes are great for many reasons. First, they complement your Raw vegan entrees, making for a delicious feast. Second, these recipes are so healthy and satisfying that they can make an entire meal of themselves. Simply make yourself a larger portion to eat, or make a couple of different sides and snacks, for an entire meal.

Side dishes are also great for introducing people to Raw. If you're trying to get your family to eat more Raw vegan food, then the next time you have a typical cooked meal with them, make the side dish Raw. Baby steps are important, and this is a great way to start. It works like a charm. You'll find your family asking you to make this kind of food more often!

JAMAICAN ME HOT AND CRAZY SAUCE

Yield 1 1/2 cups

It's so hot, a taste of this and you could be on the floor, flat on your back, staring straight up at the ceiling. *Caution:* Make at your own risk. This is very hot and spicy and reserved for the brave. You just might think you're having hot flashes when you eat this. Don't just skim past it if you're not into spicy however... Read my serving suggestions below.

1/4 cup extra virgin olive oil or hemp oil

1/4 cup + 2 tablespoons fresh orange juice

1/4 cup fresh lime juice

2 tablespoons fresh lemon juice

1 tablespoon tamari, wheat-free

1/2 teaspoon Himalayan crystal salt

1 tablespoon ground allspice

1 tablespoon fresh basil, minced

1 tablespoon dried thyme

1 tablespoon cayenne pepper

1 tablespoon raw agave nectar

1 teaspoon black pepper

1 teaspoon ground cinnamon

1/2 teaspoon ground ginger

1/2 teaspoon vanilla extract

1 habenero pepper, stemmed, seeded and finely minced*

* When handling hot peppers, put some oil on your hands to protect them or wear rubber gloves if you're highly sensitive. Immediately wash your hands, utensils, and counter top after you're done with the hot pepper. DON'T TOUCH YOUR FACE!!

Combine all of the ingredients in a glass jar and shake to mix well. Drizzle over your next vegetable side dish for a deliciously hot experience.

Serving suggestions:

- Reduce the heat a little by adding 1 - 2 tablespoons, or more, to a Raw vegan cheese recipe to really add some kick

- Use 1 - 3 tablespoons of this with some additional olive or hemp oil and use as a sauce for jicama cubes or other chopped vegetables
- Use 1 - 3 tablespoons or more, to marinate mushrooms for 15 minutes and enjoy. A little goes a long way
- Use 1 - 3 tablespoons or more, to marinate mushrooms (or other vegetables) in the dehydrator. Stir the marinade around the mushrooms and place in a dehydrator, in a dish or on a paraflex sheet, and dehydrate at 140 degrees for 45 minutes. Enjoy at that point, or lower the temperature and continue dehydrating for another 2 - 4 hours

MASHED CAULIFLOWER WITH GINGER AND GARLIC

Yield 3 - 4 servings

1 head cauliflower, florets

1/2 cup extra virgin olive oil or hemp oil

1 tablespoon garlic, pressed

1 tablespoon fresh ginger, peeled and grated

2 tablespoons fresh lemon juice

1 teaspoon raw agave nectar

1/2 teaspoon Himalayan crystal salt

black pepper to taste

Puree all of the ingredients in a food processor, fitted with the "S" blade until you reach your desired texture. Enjoy.

Variations:

- Pulse in 1/4 cup fresh basil

- Add 3/4 teaspoon paprika
- Add 1 tablespoon of curry

BLACK HUMMUS

Yield approximately 2 cups

This is such a neat hummus because it's black, making for a nice and versatile version of hummus. At Halloween, I serve this with carrots (thus black and orange) and call it *"Boo!" Halloween Hummus.*

2 medium zucchini, peeled and chopped

1/2 cup fresh lemon juice

3/4 cup black sesame raw tahini

2 cloves garlic

1 1/2 teaspoons cumin

1 teaspoon Himalayan crystal salt

1/4 teaspoon coriander

Place everything in a blender and blend until smooth and creamy. This freezes well in an airtight container.

MOUTH-WATERING DELICIOUS CRANBERRY RELISH

Yield approximately 3 cups

When fresh cranberries are in season, buy a bunch and freeze them so you can make this amazing relish any time of the year. Cranberries are loaded (and I mean *loaded*) with antioxidants, so these little beauties are important to your health.

2 cups fresh cranberries

2 - 3 oranges, peeled, pith removed, seeded and sectioned

1 kiwi, peeled and diced

1/3 cup raw agave nectar, or more to taste

2 tablespoons green onion, minced

2 tablespoons fresh lime juice

1 teaspoon fresh ginger, peeled, grated

Process the cranberries and oranges in a food processor briefly, fitted with the "S" blade. Transfer the mixture to a bowl and add the other ingredients. Stir by hand.

GREG'S MARINATED OLIVES

Yield 4 servings

These olives are great to have at your next party. Note that they need to marinate for one week prior to serving.

1/4 lb green olives

1/4 lb kalamata olives

2 cloves garlic, pressed

1 teaspoon coriander seeds

1 small lemon, cut into chunks

1 sprig fresh rosemary

(continued)

1/4 teaspoon cayenne, optional

black pepper, to taste

extra virgin olive oil or hemp oil, to cover

Place the olives on a cutting board and place a paper towel on top. Using a rolling pin or vegetable scraper (like a large spatula), gently "smash" or press down on top of the olives to get them to "crack the skins" a little. Then, take out the pits by hand. Alternatively, you can just cut them all in half with a knife, but the aforementioned method is much faster. Using a mortar and pestle, crush the coriander seeds. Cut the lemon, with its rind, into small chunks.

Put the olives, garlic, coriander seeds, lemon chunks, rosemary sprigs, and cayenne pepper into a bowl and toss together. Season with pepper to taste, if you'd like. Pack the ingredients tightly into a glass mason jar. Pour in enough olive oil to cover the olives, then seal the jar tightly.

Marinate the olives in the refrigerator for one week before serving. From time to time, gently give the jar a shake to remix the ingredients.

PARK AVENUE BEETS IN THE RAW

Yield 2 - 3 servings

If you like beets, you'll love this dish. What's not to like when beets give you vitamin C and iron, right?

2 apples, cored and shredded

2 medium beets, shredded

1/4 cup fresh parsley, chopped

(continued)

34

3 tablespoons golden raisins

3 tablespoons pine nuts

3 tablespoons flax oil or hemp oil

2 tablespoons fresh lemon juice

1 teaspoon mustard powder

1/2 teaspoon Himalayan crystal salt

pinch black pepper

Use the shredding plate with your food processor to shred the apples and the beets. Transfer them to a large bowl. Gently toss in the parsley, golden raisins, and pine nuts. Whisk together the oil, lemon juice, mustard powder, salt and pepper. Pour on the salad and toss gently to coat.

FLYING DRAGON BROCCOLI

See photo on cover and at KristensRaw.com/photos.

Yield 3 - 4 servings

I get loads of compliments about this nutritious, cancer-fighting/preventing dish.

1 medium-size head broccoli, broken into flowerets

1/3 cup extra virgin olive oil or hemp oil

2 tablespoons raw agave nectar

1 - 2 cloves garlic, pressed

1/2 teaspoon Himalayan crystal salt

2 - 3 tablespoons raisins

1/4 cup kalamata olives, chopped

Puree the broccoli, oil, agave, garlic and salt in a food processor, fitted with the "S" blade. Add more oil, or a little water, if necessary, to help puree it. Stir in the raisins. Top with the chopped olives just before serving.

Variation:

- This is delicious served with diced tomatoes on top

CINNAMON THYME VEGETABLES

Yield 2 servings

The thyme in this recipe offers a nice pungent flavor that is almost mint-like and supports the cinnamon beautifully.

The Sauce

1/2 cup extra virgin olive oil or hemp oil

1 tablespoon apple cider vinegar

1/4 teaspoon powdered ginger

1/8 teaspoon cinnamon

1/4 teaspoon paprika

1/4 teaspoon dried thyme leaves

1/8 - 1/4 teaspoon Himalayan crystal salt

pinch black pepper

The Vegetables

1 cup tomatoes, seeded and chopped

1 cup zucchini, chopped

1/2 cup carrots, thinly sliced

Blend all of the sauce ingredients together. Toss the vegetables in a bowl and pour the sauce on top. Enjoy.

FUN CHOCOLATE APPLESAUCE

Yield approximately 1 3/4 cups

Want your kids to start eating healthier? Give them this. They'll love it!

2 apples, cored and chopped

3 dates, pitted

2 tablespoons raw chocolate powder or raw carob powder

3 tablespoons raw almond butter

1/4 teaspoon cinnamon

Puree all of the ingredients in a food processor until you reach your desired texture, fitted with the "S" blade. I like mine a little on the chunky side. ☺

FRAIS FRIES

Yield Approximately 4 servings

Jicama is really the best choice when making a french fry substitute because there is a nice crispness to it. This recipe was inspired by Victoria Boutenko. These fresh, crunchy fries are fun to eat. Enjoy them dipped in my *Raw Savory Sweet Ketchup* (p. 61) for a real treat that reminds you of cooked french fries, only much healthier.

3 tablespoons hemp oil

1 clove garlic, pressed

2 teaspoons dried tarragon

1/2 teaspoon Himalayan crystal salt, or to taste

black pepper, to taste

1 pound jicama, peeled and sliced like french fries

1 tablespoon parsley, minced

Mix the oil, garlic, tarragon, salt and pepper and pour over sliced jicama. Sprinkle with the chopped parsley. Let marinate for 15 minutes and enjoy.

Serving suggestions:

- Serve this as a side dish with *Hearty Garden Burgers* (see recipe in *Kristen Suzanne's EASY Raw Vegan Entrees*)
- Eat as is... right out of the bowl.
- Dip into *Raw Savory Sweet Ketchup* (see p. 61) and *Raw Mustard* (see p. 26)

WORLDLY SPICED RICE

See photo on cover and at KristensRaw.com/photos.

Yield 4 servings

This is so easy and delicious to make, you are going to love it.

The Rice Mixture

1 butternut squash, peeled, seeded and chopped* (about 3 cups)

1 cup carrots, chopped

2 green onions, finely chopped

1/4 cup raisins

The Seasoning

2 tablespoons fresh lemon juice

2 tablespoons extra virgin olive oil or hemp oil

1 tablespoon cumin seeds

2 cloves garlic, pressed

2 teaspoons fresh ginger, peeled and grated

2 teaspoons agave nectar

1 teaspoon coriander

1 teaspoon cumin

1 teaspoon Himalayan crystal salt

3/4 teaspoon turmeric

1/4 teaspoon cayenne pepper

Use your food processor, fitted with the "S" blade, to make the rice by processing the butternut squash and carrots to the texture of rice. Place in a large bowl and toss in the green onions and raisins. Mix the seasoning ingredients in a small bowl and stir into the rice mixture.

* A vegetable peeler is perfect for peeling the squash.

Variations:

- Add 1/2 cup fresh cilantro, chopped, to the rice mixture
- Stir 1 avocado, pitted, peeled and diced into the final product (this is really good!)

MY DIRTY RICE DISH

Yield 4 servings

The Rice Mixture

1 butternut squash, peeled, seeded and chopped* (about 3 cups)

1 cup carrots, chopped

2 green onions, diced

1 red or yellow bell pepper, stemmed, seeded and diced

The Dirty Seasoning

2 tablespoons flax oil or hemp oil

2 cloves garlic, pressed

1 teaspoon dried thyme

1 teaspoon chili seasoning

1/4 teaspoon cayenne pepper

3/4 teaspoon Himalayan crystal salt, to taste

Use your food processor, fitted with the "S" blade, to make the rice by processing the butternut squash and carrots to the texture of rice. Place in a large bowl and toss in the green onions and bell pepper. Mix the Dirty Seasoning in small bowl and stir into the rice mixture.

* A vegetable peeler is perfect for peeling the squash.

Variations:

- Stir 1 avocado, pitted, peeled and diced into the final product (this is really good!)
- Add 1/4 cup raisins
- Add 1/3 cup dried cranberries

SALSA FRESHNESS

Yield 2 - 3 servings

4 medium tomatoes, (2 seeded) and all diced

2 green onions, thinly sliced

1 - 2 cloves garlic, pressed

2 tablespoons fresh cilantro, minced

1 tablespoon fresh lime juice

1/4 teaspoon Himalayan crystal salt

1 pinch cayenne pepper

Combine all of the ingredients in a bowl and enjoy.

Variation:

- Add 2 tablespoons of raw pumpkin seeds (soaked or soaked and dehydrated) or hemp seeds for extra protein and nutrition

SPICY TAHINI VEGETABLES

Yield 3 - 4 servings

Ever since I was a little girl, I've loved tahini. It's one of my favorites.

The Sauce

1/2 cup raw tahini
3 tablespoons fresh lemon juice
1/4 - 1/2 teaspoon cayenne (or to taste)
1/4 teaspoon Himalayan crystal salt
water, as needed

Vegetable options: Try any of the following suggestions with this delicious sauce and you'll be coming back for more.

4 tomatoes, chopped
1 head broccoli florets, chopped
1 head cauliflower florets, chopped
1 bunch asparagus, chopped (my favorite)

Blend all of the ingredients for the sauce together, until smooth, and drizzle over fresh vegetables (or drown the vegetables in the sauce if you're like me – ha ha).

MINTED ZUCCHINI

Yield 2 servings

Mint is another one of my favorite flavors. In this dish, it transforms plain zucchini into a cool and refreshing salad that you'll love.

2 - 3 zucchini, diced
1/4 cup red or yellow onion, diced
3 tablespoons extra virgin olive oil or hemp oil
1 tablespoon fresh lime juice
1 tablespoon fresh mint, minced
pinch Himalayan crystal salt, or more to taste
black pepper, to taste

Mix all of the ingredients together in a bowl and enjoy.

THE GREATEST HUMMUS IN THE WORLD

Yield 2 cups

Goodness, I love this delicious, super healthy dip. It's phenomenal!

2 medium zucchini, peeled and chopped
3/4 cup raw tahini
1/3 cup fresh lemon juice, more if needed
2 cloves garlic

(continued)

1 1/2 teaspoons cumin

1/2 teaspoon coriander

1 teaspoon Himalayan crystal salt

1/2 teaspoon fresh lemon zest

1/4 cup fresh basil, chopped

Place everything in a blender, except the fresh basil, and blend until smooth and creamy. Pulse in the fresh basil. This freezes well in an airtight container.

TAHINI GARDEN MEDLEY

Yield 4 servings

This dish will quickly become a favorite in your household, I'm sure of it. You'll get many uses out of this sauce.

The Tahini-Parsley Sauce

1/2 cup water

1/2 cup fresh lemon juice

2 tablespoons raw tahini

1 clove garlic

1 teaspoon cumin

1/4 teaspoon Himalayan crystal salt

1/2 teaspoon allspice

pinch black pepper

1 cup parsley, chopped

The Garden Medley

   3 medium zucchini, sliced into 1/2 inch rounds

   1 1/2 cups tomatoes, chopped

   3/4 cup mushrooms, sliced

   1/4 cup fennel, sliced

   1/4 cup red onions, diced

To make the sauce, blend all of the ingredients together, except the parsley. Pulse in the parsley. Place all of the vegetables in a large bowl. Pour the Tahini-Parsley Sauce on top. Toss to coat. Enjoy!

SUPER MEDLEY WITH BRAVO GARLIC SAUCE

Yield 2 servings

This is a *super* medley because the broccoli, red bell pepper, and carrots bring you tons of nutrients. And the taste? Oh my gosh... so delicious! I make this all the time.

The Sauce

   1/3 cup extra virgin olive oil

   1 1/2 tablespoons tamari, wheat-free

   1 clove garlic, pressed

   Juice from 1 lime

   1/2 teaspoon garlic powder

   1/2 teaspoon onion powder

   pinch black pepper

The Vegetables

> 1 1/2 cups broccoli florets, chopped
> 1 cup red bell pepper, destemmed, seeded, and diced
> 2/3 cup sliced carrots

In a small bowl, whisk together the olive oil, tamari, fresh garlic, lime juice, garlic powder, onion powder, and pepper. Put the vegetables in a medium bowl and pour the sauce over them. Toss to mix and let marinate 30 minutes, stirring occasionally. Or, warm in a dehydrator for 45 minutes at 130 degrees.

FRESH VEGETABLE CONFETTI

Yield 2 servings

This is always a real crowd pleaser.

The Spicy Tahini and Cilantro Sauce

> 1/4 cup water
> 1/4 cup fresh lemon juice
> 2 tablespoons raw tahini
> 1 clove garlic
> 1/2 teaspoon cumin
> 1/8 - 1/4 teaspoon cayenne
> pinch Himalayan crystal salt
> 1/2 cup cilantro, chopped

To make the sauce, blend all of the ingredients together, except the cilantro. Pulse in the cilantro.

The Confetti

> 1 medium carrot, diced
>
> 1 red bell pepper, stemmed, seeded, and diced
>
> 1 yellow bell pepper, stemmed, seeded, and diced
>
> 1 zucchini, diced

Mix the ingredients for the confetti in a bowl. Pour the Spicy Tahini and Cilantro Sauce over the diced confetti and toss to coat. Store any extra sauce in an air-tight container in the refrigerator for up to 5 days.

TUSCAN SUN-DRIED TOMATO PESTO

See photo at KristensRaw.com/photos.

Yield approximately 1 cup

> This is truly terrific!
>
> 1 cup sun-dried tomatoes, soaked 1 - 2 hours, reserve soak water
>
> 1/2 cup fresh basil, packed
>
> 1/4 cup pine nuts
>
> 1 teaspoon garlic, pressed
>
> 1 teaspoon Himalayan crystal salt
>
> 2 tablespoons fresh lemon juice
>
> 1/3 cup extra virgin olive oil

In a food processor, fitted with the "S" blade, combine all of the ingredients except the olive oil, adding a little of the sun-dried tomato "soak" water, if necessary. While the mixture is pureeing, add the olive oil. This freezes well.

Serving suggestions:

- Stuff 1/2 of a seeded bell pepper (yellow or orange are especially beautiful)
- Serve on top of zucchini angel hair pasta for a real treat
- Stuff inside a beet or turnip rawvioli (see recipes in *Kristen Suzanne's EASY Raw Vegan Entrees*)
- Use this to flavor a simple salad dressing by blending 2 tablespoons of it with some olive oil, a little water, and a squeeze of citrus.

MARINATED CREMINI MUSHROOMS AND ARUGULA

Yield 2 large servings

This dish is perfect for anyone who is craving food that is cooked. The marinated mushrooms take on a wonderfully dense and "cooked-like" texture. The peppery flavor from the arugula and the earthy flavor of the marinated mushrooms make this dish one of the best.

1 bunch of arugula
2 cups sliced cremini mushrooms

The Marinade

1/2 cup extra virgin olive oil

2 tablespoons fresh lemon juice

1 tablespoon tamari, wheat-free

1 clove garlic, pressed

pinch cayenne, optional

Season with black pepper

Whisk together the ingredients for the marinade. Toss the marinade with the thinly sliced cremini mushrooms. Let them sit for 15 minutes and then toss them gently with the arugula.

Serving suggestions:

- If you have a dehydrator, here is a great place to use it. After marinating the mushrooms, dehydrate them at 140 degrees for about 30 - 45 minutes, then mix them with the salad.
- Chop the mushrooms into small pieces, instead of slices, and stuff the marinated mushrooms into the half of a seeded bell pepper or tomato.

Variations:

- Substitute the arugula for fresh spinach
- Add 2 tomatoes, chopped, just before serving
- Add fresh chopped basil

ROSE GARDEN RICE

Yield 4 - 6 servings

1 butternut squash, peeled, seeded and chopped (about 3 cups)

1 cup carrots, chopped

1 cup pecans or walnuts, soaked 6 - 8 hours, drained and rinsed

1/2 teaspoon cardamom, ground

2 teaspoons rose water*

zest of 1 orange

1/4 teaspoon Himalayan crystal salt

3/4 cup dates, pitted and chopped

1/2 cup fresh parsley, chopped

Using a food processor, fitted with the "S" blade, pulse the squash and carrots until you get a "rice" texture. Set aside in a large bowl. Next, place the nuts, cardamom, rose water, orange zest and salt in the food processor and grind to a texture that is coarsely ground. Stir this into the squash "rice." Add the dates and parsley. Toss well to mix.

* You can find rose water, as well as orange blossom water, in most Middle Eastern markets, online, and in some Whole Foods Markets.

Variations:

- Substitute dried cranberries or raisins for the dates
- For a real treat, use pistachios or macadamia nuts (you don't have to soak these) instead of pecans or walnuts
- Substitute the rose water for orange blossom water (and change the name of it, if serving to others ☺)

MINTED ORANGE CAULIFLOWER

See photo at KristensRaw.com/photos.

Yield 3 - 4 servings

Cauliflower was never fun to eat for me, so I had to come up with something that would entice me to eat it. I did just that with this recipe.

> 1 medium-size head of cauliflower, broken into flowerets
>
> 1 1/2 cups carrots, chopped
>
> 1/3 cup extra virgin olive oil or hemp oil
>
> zest from one fresh orange
>
> 2 - 3 tablespoons raw agave nectar
>
> 2 tablespoons apple cider vinegar
>
> 2 teaspoons fresh ginger, peeled and grated
>
> 1 tablespoon orange blossom water*
>
> 1/2 teaspoon Himalayan crystal salt, or more to taste
>
> 1/4 teaspoon black pepper, or more to taste
>
> 1/4 cup fresh mint leaves, chopped

Lightly puree all of the ingredients, except for the mint, in a food processor, fitted with the "S" blade. Pulse in the mint leaves.

* You can find orange blossom water in most Middle Eastern markets, online, and in some Whole Foods Markets.

SUPER-CAULIFLOWER WITH TAHINI

Yield 4 servings

The Tahini-Parsley Sauce

1/2 cup water

1/2 cup fresh lemon juice

2 tablespoons raw tahini

1 clove garlic

1 teaspoon cumin

1/2 teaspoon allspice

1/4 teaspoon Himalayan crystal salt

pinch black pepper

1 cup parsley, chopped

The Dish

1 head cauliflower, florets

3/4 cup tahini and parsley sauce

1/2 cup *My Basic Raw Mayonnaise* (see p. 27)

1/4 cup raisins

To make the sauce, blend all of the ingredients together, except the parsley. Pulse in the parsley. Place the cauliflower, Tahini-Parsley Sauce and Raw mayonnaise in a food processor, fitted with the "S" blade, and process until almost pureed. Stir in the raisins. Enjoy this super healthy dish!

CHAPTER 3

SPREADS, DIPS & SAUCES

It's smart to always have some kind of Raw vegan spread, dip, or sauce on hand in the refrigerator. This way you'll always have a quick snack, which is very important for people with a busy lifestyle. All you have to do is grab some carrots, celery or any veggie and enjoy an easy and delicious snack. I make it a point to make 1 - 2 different Raw vegan spreads, dips or sauces every Sunday so I have them for the week ahead. Note: many of these spreads and dips freeze well, so it's smart to have some of these "ready-to-thaw" waiting in your freezer. Remember, one of the keys to easily living the Raw vegan lifestyle is having these foods already made for yourself.

EASY PINE-HEMP DIPPING SAUCE

Yield approximately 3/4 cup

   1/4 cup pine nuts, soaked 1 hour, drained and rinsed

   1/4 cup hemp seeds

   2 tablespoons hemp oil or olive oil

   1/4 cup water, more if needed

   2 tablespoons fresh lemon juice

   1 clove garlic

   (continued)

1/4 - 1/2 teaspoon Himalayan crystal salt, or more to taste

black pepper, to taste

1 tablespoon fresh herb of your choice, chopped

Blend all of the ingredients, except the fresh herb, until smooth and creamy. Pulse in the fresh herb. This freezes well.

Serving suggestion:

- Use this as a creamy dressing or as a fabulous dipping sauce for your vegetables

KRISTEN SUZANNE'S FAMOUS OLIVE TAPENADE

Yield approx 4 cups

This is one of my husband's favorite dishes. I make it every year on his birthday.

2 cups kalamata olives, pitted

1 cup green olives, pitted

1/3 cup capers

3 tablespoons currants or (chopped) golden raisins or Turkish apricots

1/4 bunch cilantro (or basil), chopped

2 Serrano red peppers, stemmed and seeded

1 tablespoon garlic, pressed

1 teaspoon fresh lemon juice

(continued)

3 tablespoons flax oil or hemp oil

3 tablespoons extra virgin olive oil

1 orange bell pepper, stemmed, seeded and diced

Place all of the ingredients, except both of the oils and the orange bell pepper, in a food processor, fitted with the "S" blade, and process until the olives are coarsely chopped. Briefly pulse the food processor while streaming the oils in. Transfer to a bowl and stir in the minced orange bell pepper.

GIDDEE-UP AVOCADO DIP

Yield approximately 2 cups

This is such a unique and delicious dip.

2 stalks celery, chopped

2 tablespoons fresh lime juice

1 tablespoon water

1 tablespoon extra virgin olive oil*

1 ripe avocado, pitted and peeled

2 tablespoons fresh horseradish, peeled and grated**

1 clove garlic

1 scallion (white and green parts), minced

1/2 teaspoon Himalayan crystal salt

Blend all of the ingredients together until creamy using a blender.

* You can substitute the olive oil for 1 tablespoon of water, giving a total of 2 tablespoons water in the recipe.

** To prepare the horseradish, get fresh horseradish root in your grocery store's produce section. Cut off the peel with a knife (or peel with a vegetable peeler). Grate the desired amount. If you can't find fresh horseradish, you can substitute with prepared horseradish in a jar (this is not raw) and start with 1 tablespoon. Taste it and see if you'd like to add more.

ORANGE SUNSET SALSA

Yield 2 - 3 servings

> 4 medium tomatoes, (2 seeded) and all diced
>
> 2 oranges, peeled, pith removed, seeded, sectioned and chopped
>
> 2 green onions, thinly sliced
>
> 2 tablespoons cilantro, minced
>
> 2 tablespoons fresh lime juice
>
> 1 clove garlic, pressed
>
> 3/4 teaspoon fresh ginger, peeled and grated
>
> 1/4 teaspoon Himalayan crystal salt
>
> 1 pinch cayenne pepper

Combine all of the ingredients in a bowl and enjoy.

Variations:

- Add 3 dates, pitted and chopped
- Add 1/4 cup pecans, chopped

SWEET ROSE SAUCE

Yield approximately 1/2 cup

This sauce is great for both sweet dessert dishes and savory vegetable dishes. It's probably not something you'd eat by itself (unless you're my mom, because she loves the flavor of roses), so when tasting it after you prepare it, make sure to taste it with a fruit or vegetable that it'll be served with. For a worldly experience, try this drizzled over chopped red onions and other vegetables.

1/2 cup dates, pitted, packed

2 tablespoons fresh lemon juice

2 - 3 teaspoons rose water, depending on the strength of rose flavor you desire*

1/2 cup water, more if desired

In a food processor, fitted with the "S" blade, puree the dates with the lemon juice and rose water, adding enough water to make a creamy sauce.

* You can find rose water at most Middle Eastern markets, online, and in some Whole Foods Markets.

SEA SIDE COTTAGE SPREAD

Yield 1 1/4 cup

This is one of my favorite spreads to serve with fresh organic vegetables or flax crackers. It's delicious!

2/3 cup raw cashews, soaked 1 - 2 hours, drained and rinsed

1 tablespoon onion, chopped

(continued)

2 tablespoons celery, minced

1 tablespoon raw tahini

2 tablespoons fresh lemon juice

2 teaspoons tamari, wheat-free

1 clove garlic

1 teaspoon kelp, or more to taste

1/4 teaspoon Himalayan crystal salt

1/4 teaspoon white pepper

1/4 cup water, as needed

Place all of the ingredients in a blender and blend until smooth and creamy, adding the water, as needed. Taste it and decide whether you'd like more "sea side" flavor. If so, add more kelp. This freezes well.

Serving suggestions:

- Fabulous as a dip for vegetable crudités
- Perfect inside a collard green wrap sandwich

Variation:

- For a lower fat version, use only 1/2 cup cashews (pre-soak measurement) and add 1 small zucchini before blending

LIGHT-N-LIVELY TAHINI PARSLEY DRESSING

Yield approximately 1 3/4 cup

This is fragrant, fresh, lively and vibrant. Add to that the fact that it's simple to make and can be used as a nice light dressing on salad or poured onto a hearty vegetable dish.

1/2 cup water

1/4 cup fresh lemon juice

1/4 cup fresh lime juice

2 1/2 tablespoons raw tahini

1 clove garlic

1 teaspoon cumin

1/2 teaspoon allspice

1/4 teaspoon Himalayan crystal salt (or more)

1/4 teaspoon coriander

pinch black pepper

1 cup parsley, chopped

Blend all of the ingredients together, except the parsley, until smooth. Pulse in the parsley.

ONE-STOP-SHOP SPREAD

Yield 1 1/2 cup

Next time you want a spread or dip that covers all the bases, this is it. It's like mayo, ketchup, and mustard all in one.

1 1/4 cup *Crème Fraiche* (see p. 25)

1 medium zucchini, peeled and chopped

2 tablespoons *Raw Mustard* (see p. 26)

2 tablespoons *Raw Savory Sweet Ketchup* (see p. 61)

Blend all of the ingredients together until creamy. Spread on veggies, bread, and crackers or just lick it off your fingers! This freezes well.

RED MOUNTAIN SEASONED PECAN SAUCE

Yield approximately 1 cup

This is one of my favorite sauces because of its beautiful unique flavors and pretty color. Not to mention it's so simple to make!

1/2 cup pecans, soaked 6 hours, drained and rinsed
1 red bell pepper, stemmed, seeded and chopped
1/4 cup fresh lemon juice
1 clove garlic
1/2 tablespoon extra virgin olive oil
1/2 tablespoon cumin
1/2 tablespoon ground coriander
1/2 tablespoon paprika
1/4 teaspoon Himalayan crystal salt
1/8 teaspoon cayenne pepper
water, as needed

Blend all of the ingredients together until creamy. Serve with vegetables.

ESSENCE DE L'ORANGE DATE SAUCE

Yield approximately 1/2 cup

1/4 cup dates, pitted and packed

Juice of 1 lemon or lime

2 tablespoons orange blossom water, or more depending on preference*

1/2 cup water

In a food processor, fitted with the "S" blade, puree the dates with the lemon juice, orange blossom water, and water to make a creamy sauce.

* This is available at most Middle Eastern markets, online, and in some Whole Food Markets.

Serving suggestion:

- Enjoy this sauce on fresh fruit or vegetables

Variation:

- Add various seasonings such as cinnamon, allspice, cumin, fresh mint, etc. For seasonings, I'd start with approximately one pinch and tasting as you go, adding more if desired. For fresh herbs, I'd start with 2 teaspoons.

RAW SAVORY SWEET KETCHUP

Yield 2 1/2 cups

3/4 cup fresh tomatoes, chopped

1 cup sun-dried tomatoes, soaked 1 - 2 hours in just enough water to cover, reserve soak water

(continued)

1 tablespoon apple cider vinegar

2 cloves garlic

2 1/2 teaspoons ginger, peeled and grated

2 - 3 dates, pitted or 2 tablespoons raisins

3 - 4 tablespoons raw agave nectar

2 tablespoons extra virgin olive oil

1 teaspoon onion powder

1 teaspoon Himalayan crystal salt

pinch black pepper

1 - 2 tablespoons of water, if needed

Blend all of the ingredients, including the tomato soak water, until smooth. Ketchup will last up to one week stored in a glass jar in the refrigerator. Or, freeze for 24 hours in ice cube trays. Then, transfer the frozen cubes to a freezer bag or glass jar. Take them out one at a time, as needed.

CHEEZY NACHO SAUCE

Yield approximately 2 cups

1/2 cup pine nuts, soaked 1 hour, drained and rinsed

1/2 sunflower seeds, soaked 4 - 6 hours, drained and rinsed

1/2 cup water

1 red bell pepper, stemmed, seeded and chopped

1 carrot, chopped

2 cloves garlic

2 tablespoons nutritional yeast

(continued)

1 tablespoon fresh lemon juice

1 teaspoon lime juice, optional

1 teaspoon Himalayan crystal salt

1/4 teaspoon cayenne pepper (more or less depending on how spicy you like it)

2 - 3 teaspoons Mexican seasoning

Put all of the ingredients in a blender and blend until smooth and creamy. Cheezy Nacho Sauce can be stored in the refrigerator for up to five days. This freezes pretty well.

Serving suggestions:

- This sauce is wonderful drenching a raw burrito wrapped in a collard green topped with fresh tomato salsa. It's so satisfying.
- Use as a sauce for dipping fresh veggies, or make a thicker version with less water and use as a dip for corn chips.
- This also makes a delicious dressing on a hearty salad with romaine lettuce!

GARLIC MINT PESTO-LIKE SAUCE

Yield approximately 3/4 - 1 cup

There are no nuts in this pesto-like sauce, which makes it extra creamy and smooth. The mint is very clean, making it especially refreshing when the weather is hot outside. One of my favorite ways to enjoy this sauce is drizzled over fresh zucchini pasta.

1/2 bunch fresh parsley, chopped

1/2 bunch fresh mint, chopped

1 Serrano red pepper, whole (stem removed)

2 tablespoons raw agave nectar

2 - 3 garlic cloves, pressed

1/2 teaspoon Himalayan crystal salt

1/8 teaspoon black pepper

3/4 cup extra virgin olive oil

In your food processor, fitted with the "S" blade, place all of the ingredients except the olive oil, and puree. While food processor is still running, slowly add the olive oil. Store in an airtight container (glass mason jar works best) until you're ready to use.

LEMON MINT DIP

Yield 4 servings

This is one of the most refreshing dips I make. It's a terrific way to dress up plain veggies and give them pizazz. (Veggies never tasted so good!)

2 zucchini, chopped

3 tablespoons fresh lemon juice

3 tablespoons extra virgin olive oil

1 clove garlic

zest of 1 fresh lemon

1 teaspoon cumin

(continued)

1/4 teaspoon dried thyme

1/4 teaspoon Himalayan crystal salt

pinch black pepper

1/4 cup fresh mint, chopped

Blend all of the ingredients, except the mint, until smooth. Pulse in the chopped mint.

GINGER HUMMUS

Yield approximately 2 1/2 cups

I love ginger because it helps improve circulation and digestion, making this variation on hummus extra nutritious.

1 large zucchini, peeled and chopped

2/3 cup raw tahini*

1/3 cup fresh lemon juice, more if necessary

1 1/2 tablespoons fresh grated ginger, packed

1 teaspoon cumin

1/2 teaspoon coriander

1 teaspoon Himalayan crystal salt

1/2 teaspoon fresh lemon zest

dash cinnamon

Blend all of the ingredients until smooth in your blender. Ginger Hummus will keep in an airtight container in your refrigerator for up to five days. This also freezes well.

Serving suggestion:

- Ginger Hummus is scrumptious with fresh chopped vegetables.

* Depending on the texture of the raw tahini you use, your recipe can turn out either with a sauce texture or thicker like a dip.

HERBIN' RANCH DIP

See photo at KristensRaw.com/photos.

Yield 1 1/2 cups

This is the one of the most nutritious, delicious ways to have ranch dip, but without guilt. I love serving this dip at summer picnics with vegetable crudités or as a dressing on your favorite greens.*

1/2 cup raw cashews, unsoaked

1/2 cup raw pine nuts, unsoaked

1 zucchini, peeled and chopped

1 tablespoon extra virgin coconut oil

3 tablespoons fresh lemon juice

1 clove garlic

1 teaspoon onion powder

1 teaspoon Himalayan crystal salt

1/2 teaspoon tarragon

1/8 teaspoon white pepper

1/4 cup fresh basil, not packed

1/4 cup fresh dill, not packed

Blend all of the ingredients, except the fresh basil and dill, until creamy and smooth. Pulse in the basil and dill. This will stay fresh for 4 - 5 days when stored in an airtight container (mason jar works great) in the refrigerator. This dip also freezes well.

* To make this as a dressing, simply add a little water until you reach the desired consistency. The picture on my website shows this recipe used as a dressing.

GREEN MONSTER MASH

Yield 1 1/2 cups

This is truly one of the most delicious and nutritious dips ever (loaded with fiber, vitamins and minerals). The chewy sun-dried tomatoes make each bite extra heavenly and exciting. This recipe can be eaten on its own, accompanied by sliced cucumbers or flax crackers, or enjoyed as a side dish for your next dinner.

2 medium avocados, pitted and peeled

2 cups spinach, packed

3 tablespoons fresh lime juice

1 clove garlic, chopped

1 teaspoon onion powder

1 teaspoon dried oregano

1/2 teaspoon dried basil

1/2 teaspoon Himalayan crystal salt

1 cup sun-dried tomatoes, soaked 30 - 45 minutes, drained and chopped

Process all of the ingredients, except the sun-dried tomatoes, using a food processor, fitted with the "S" blade, until somewhat creamy, yet still a little chunky. Add the soaked and chopped sun-dried tomatoes and pulse a few times to mix them in. Green Monster Mash will stay fresh for up to two days when stored in an airtight container in the refrigerator.

CREAMY ZINGER GARLIC SPREAD

See photo at KristensRaw.com/photos.

Yield 1 1/2 cups

This is yet another favorite in our household. We love spreading it onto crunchy Raw crackers, but it's also wonderful as a dip for vegetables. Yum!

> 1 cup cashews, macadamia or pine nuts (or a mix) soaked 1 hour, drained and rinsed
>
> 1 large clove garlic
>
> 1 tablespoon Garlic Red Pepper Miso*
>
> 1 tablespoon light miso
>
> 1 tablespoon fresh lemon juice
>
> 1 tablespoon extra virgin coconut oil
>
> a little water, if needed to help blend

Blend all of the ingredients until creamy in your blender (or food processor) and enjoy this gourmet-flavored deliciousness. Creamy Zinger Garlic Spread will stay fresh for up to five days in your refrigerator (stored in an airtight container). It also freezes great.

Variation:

- GREAT TIP: For those watching your nut intake, here is a tip for reducing the fat in spreads such as this, without compromising the exquisite experience. Replace half of the nuts with 1 - 2 zucchini (peeled). Keep in mind that fat helps mellow flavors, so by reducing the fat, you might need to reduce a few of the more "flavorful" ingredients. For example, I'd start with 1/2 tablespoon of each of the miso(s) and look for a clove of garlic that isn't too big. Start small because you can always add more, if desired.

* This wonderful miso is soy-free and available from South River Miso (SouthRiverMiso.com).

CHAPTER 4

SNACKS

At one time or another, we've all found ourselves staring into a refrigerator like a deer in headlights... you're hungry and you have the munchies but you just don't know what to eat. These recipes are perfect for that!

GROOVIN' "FRUI-TEA" SWEET SEEDS

Yield approximately 1 cup

These are the perfect snack for munching on during a movie.

> 1 cup mixed pumpkin seeds and sunflower seeds, soaked 6 - 8 hours in a strongly brewed, organic fruit-flavored herbal tea*, drained
>
> 2 tablespoons raw agave nectar
>
> 1 teaspoon vanilla extract
>
> 3/4 teaspoon ground ginger
>
> 1/8 teaspoon Himalayan crystal salt

* To make fruit flavored tea, warm some water and add to a bowl with a couple of your favorite fruit-flavored tea bags. Let it sit on your counter for a couple of hours to increase the strength. You can set it in the sun to help, too.

Once the tea is made, remove the tea bags and add the seeds to the bowl to soak, making sure there is enough water/tea to cover them. After 6 - 8 hours, drain the seeds and add the remaining ingredients to the seeds and stir. Spread them out on a paraflex dehydrator tray and dehydrate the seeds at 140 degrees for about an hour. Then, reduce the temperature to 105 degrees and dehydrate another 12 - 24 hours or until they're dry. Enjoy!

SIMPLY SWEET PUMPKIN SEEDS

Yield approximately 1 cup

> 1 cup pumpkin seeds, soaked 6 - 8 hours, drained and rinsed
>
> 2 tablespoons raw agave nectar
>
> 1/2 teaspoon cinnamon
>
> 1/4 teaspoon nutmeg
>
> 1/8 teaspoon Himalayan crystal salt

Place the seeds in a bowl and stir in the remaining ingredients. Spread them out on a paraflex dehydrator tray and dehydrate the seeds at 140 degrees for about an hour. Reduce the temperature to 105 degrees and dehydrate another 12 - 24 hours or until they're dry.

SWEET VANILLA RAIN SUNFLOWER SEEDS

Yield approximately 1 cup

These are so delicious on their own or as a cereal with fresh creamy nut milk or topped on Raw vegan ice cream or on top of a salad. Make a few batches because they last a long time and freeze great!

> 1 cup sunflower seeds, soaked 6 - 8 hours, drained and rinsed
>
> 2 tablespoons yacon syrup or raw agave nectar
>
> 1/2 teaspoon vanilla
>
> 1/2 teaspoon cinnamon
>
> 1/4 teaspoon nutmeg
>
> 1/8 teaspoon Himalayan crystal salt

Place the seeds in a bowl and stir in the remaining ingredients. Spread them out on a paraflex dehydrator tray and dehydrate at 140 degrees for about an hour. Reduce the temperature to 105 degrees and dehydrate another 12 - 24 hours or until they're dry.

CAJUN SPICE NUTS

The Seasoning Mix

Yield 1 1/4 cup

> 1/4 cup + 2 tablespoons paprika
>
> 1 1/2 tablespoons Himalayan crystal salt
>
> 2 tablespoons onion powder
>
> 2 tablespoons garlic powder
>
> 2 tablespoons cayenne pepper
>
> 1 1/2 tablespoons white pepper

(continued)

1 1/2 tablespoons black pepper

1 1/2 tablespoons dried thyme leaves

1 1/2 tablespoons dried oregano leaves

In a small bowl, whisk all of the ingredients together. Store in a mason jar (this will keep for up to six months) and use for seasoning Raw vegan cheeses, nuts and seeds, salad dressings, veggies and more.

The Cajun Spice Pecans

Yield 1 cup

1 cup pecans, soaked 4 - 6 hours, drained and rinsed

2 tablespoons Cajun Spice Mix

1 tablespoon fresh lime juice

Toss the soaked pecans in the lime juice and spice mixture. Spread them out on a paraflex dehydrator tray and dehydrate at 140 degrees for about an hour. Reduce the temperature to 105 degrees and dehydrate another 12 - 24 hours, or until they're dry.

SEEDS OF ZEN

Yield approximately 1 cup

1 cup mixed pumpkin seeds and sunflower seeds, soaked 6 - 8 hours in strongly brewed green tea*

1 tablespoon tamari, wheat-free

(continued)

1 teaspoon cumin

1 teaspoon ground ginger

1/2 teaspoon paprika

* To make your green tea, warm some water and add to a bowl with a couple of your favorite organic green tea bags. Let the tea sit for a couple of hours to increase in strength. You can set it on your porch in the sun, too.

Once the tea is made, remove the tea bags or tea leaves and add the seeds to the bowl to soak, making sure there is enough water/tea to cover them. After 6 - 8 hours, drain the seeds and add the remaining ingredients to the seeds and stir.

Spread out on a paraflex dehydrator tray and dehydrate the seeds at 140 degrees for about an hour. Reduce the temperature to 105 degrees and dehydrate another 12 - 24 hours or until they're dry.

ZUCCHINI MUNCHIES

Yield approximately 1 cup

These are always great to have around, particularly when you just want to munch on a little something.

2 medium zucchini

3 tablespoons extra virgin olive oil, more if needed

2 tablespoons fresh lemon juice, more if needed

1 clove garlic, pressed

1/4 teaspoon cumin

(continued)

1/2 teaspoon Himalayan crystal salt

1/8 teaspoon cayenne

1/8 teaspoon paprika

1/4 bunch fresh parsley, chopped

Slice the zucchini into thin rounds, using a mandoline or V-slicer (or knife) and place them in a bowl with the other ingredients, making sure to coat all the pieces. Wait 10 - 20 minutes.

Transfer them (shake off any excess oil first) to a dehydrator tray and lay them on it in a single layer without overlapping.

Dehydrate them at 140 degrees for an hour. Lower the temperature to 105 degrees and continue dehydrating until you reach the desired texture (anywhere from 10 - 24 hours or more, depending on their thickness).

CHAPTER 5

Breakfast

Eggs and sausage every morning is an express ticket to the graveyard! Eating the world's healthiest breakfast food is extremely satisfying and delicious, once you know some basic recipes. The following are SUPER EASY ways to serve the TRUE breakfast of champions!

ROMANTIC PEACH CHUTNEY

Yield 2 servings

I adore this recipe. I like this for breakfast topped on Raw vegan oatmeal... *delicious!* (See *Good Ol' Oatmeal*, page 79.) I also sometimes have it as a great side dish at dinner.

- 1/4 cup raw agave nectar
- 2 tablespoons apple cider vinegar
- 1 teaspoon fresh ginger, peeled and grated
- 1/4 teaspoon mustard powder
- 1/8 teaspoon Himalayan crystal salt, or more to taste
- 3 peaches, pitted, and chopped

Blend the agave, apple cider vinegar, ginger, mustard powder, and salt in a blender. Pour over the peaches and toss well to coat.

Variations:

- This is great with 1 peach and 1 green apple, or all apples and call it "Apple Chutney"
- Try this with tomatoes and/or red bell peppers

THE DANCING ROOTS

Yield 3 cups

This dish is really fun. Just try it and see. It's an easy and awesome way to get more nutrients from delicious root vegetables into your diet. And... kids love it!

2 cups carrots, chopped

1 1/2 cups beet, chopped

1 1/2 tablespoons raw agave nectar

1/2 cup fresh orange juice

1/4 teaspoon Himalayan crystal salt

Puree all of the ingredients, using a food processor, fitted with the "S" blade. Enjoy this with your loved one at breakfast or eat it by yourself! ☺

Variations:

- Add 1/2 cup chopped walnuts, pecans or hemp seeds
- Pulse in 1/4 cup of fresh mint, chopped
- Add 1/4 cup raisins or dates (pitted and chopped) for fun flavor and texture

Additional serving suggestions:

- For a fabulous lunch dish, spoon this onto a bed of hearty salad greens
- Stuff marinated mushrooms with this delish mixture as a side dish to your next dinner

GOOD OL' OATMEAL

Yield approximately 1 cup

This recipe is delicious, easy and fun! Try it for breakfast tomorrow.

> 1/3 cup macadamia or Brazil nuts, unsoaked
>
> 1 cup fresh rolled oats, soaked overnight, drained and rinsed*
>
> 1 banana, peeled, or 1 apple, cored and chopped
>
> 2 tablespoons raw agave nectar
>
> 1/2 teaspoon cinnamon
>
> pinch Himalayan crystal salt
>
> 2 tablespoons raisins

Grind the nuts until they're coarsely ground, using a food processor, fitted with the "S" blade. Add the remaining ingredients, and process until you reach your desired texture. Stored in an airtight container, Good Ol' Oatmeal will keep for up to two days, but it's best eaten fresh after making.

For extra comfort and deliciousness: warm this in the dehydrator at 125 degrees for approximately 20 - 30 minutes.

* NaturalZing.com offers 100% organic fresh rolled oats that are cold rolled in small batches with special equipment to maintain nutrients.

CREAMY BREAKFAST MOUSSE

See photo at KristensRaw.com/photos.

Yield approximately 1 cup (1 - 2 servings)

This is a delightful way to get loads of vitamins into your diet first thing in the morning. It's for those days that you want something more substantial than green juice or smoothies. Truth be told... I love this as a snack or dessert, too. It goes beyond just breakfast time.

I made this in one of my classes recently and I received tons of praise for it.

1 avocado, peeled and pitted

Juice of 1 lemon

Juice of 1 orange

2 tablespoons raw agave nectar

1/4 teaspoon almond extract

1 banana (sliced) and/or mango (diced)

Blend all of the ingredients, except the banana or mango, until smooth. Transfer to a bowl and stir in the banana or mango (or simply top the Creamy Breakfast Mousse with it). This dish is best served right after preparing it.

CARNIVAL CARAMEL APPLE BREAKFAST

Yield 2 servings

It tastes just like a caramel apple you get at the carnival, but healthy enough to have for breakfast! Every kid I know loves this dish... including me!

2 large apples, cored and chopped

1/4 cup raw almond butter

4 - 5 soft dates, pitted

Using a food processor, fitted with the "S" blade, process the ingredients until you reach your desired texture... chunky or saucy.

SUNNY MORNING CEREAL

Yield 1 serving

Life would not be complete without cereal, so I had to create a delicious raw vegan recipe for one.

1 cup *Buckies**

2 tablespoons hemp seeds

2 tablespoons raisins or 2 dates, pitted and chopped

1 tablespoon pumpkin seeds

1/2 - 3/4 cup raw *Nut/Seed Milk* (see p. 25)

Place all of the ingredients in a bowl and enjoy. For an extra jump start to your morning, make the milk Raw *chocolate* milk. This is a favorite among kids... and *me!*
Variation:

- Add 1/2 cup of berries, sliced banana, or chopped apple

* To make your *Buckies*, soak raw buckwheat overnight (make a lot, like 4 cups or more, so you have plenty on hand). Drain them the next morning and give them a quick rinse. Place

them in a colander over a bowl. Allow to sprout for two days, rinsing and draining 1 – 2 times daily. Dehydrate your sprouted *Buckies* at 105 degrees until dry (usually 6 – 10 hours). Leftover *Buckies* will keep for up to six months when stored in a glass mason jar in your refrigerator.

Printed in the United Kingdom by
Lightning Source UK Ltd., Milton Keynes
140743UK00001B/155/P